GARLIC

Uses & Medicinal Properties of the Herbal Wonder

GW00702439

Dr. Rajeev Sharma

MANOJ PUBLICATIONS

© *All Rights Reserved*

Publishers:

Manoj Publications
761, Main Road, Burari, Delhi-110084
Ph: 27611116, 27611349, Fax: 27611546
Mobile: 9868112194
E-mail: *info@manojpublications.com*
Website: *www.manojpublications.com*

Showroom:

Manoj Publications
1583-84, Dariba Kalan, Chandni Chowk
Delhi-110006
Ph.: 23262174, 23268216, Mob.: 9818753569

ISBN : 978-81-310-0739-6

Third Edition : 2011

₹ 40

Printers:
Jai Maya Offset
Jhilmil Industrial Area, Delhi-110095

Garlic : Dr. Rajeev Sharma

PREFACE

Garlic is one of the oldest known medicinal plants, and it's been credited with fighting heart disease, lowering blood pressure and helping to fight off colds.

The therapeutic qualities of garlic are nothing new. Sanskrit records reveal that garlic remedies were pressed into service in India 5,000 years ago, while Chinese medicine has recognised garlic's powers for over 3,000 years. Although Alexander Fleming's discovery of penicillin in 1928 largely took over from garlic, World War I overwhelmed the capacity and garlic was again, the antibiotic of choice.

When cloves are chewed, crushed or cut, they release a sulphur-bearing compound called allicin—the chemical that gives garlic its pungent taste and smell. And it's the allicin that scientists have discovered is the magic ingredient thought to be responsible for garlic's therapeutic qualities.

There is a sulfur agent found in garlic's essential oils that makes it a potent disinfectant and a good defence for killing germs in the body. Garlic also contains calcium, selenium , zinc and potassium. It helps keep blood clots from forming in the blood vessels, and from having plaque building up in cornorary artieries.

In this book the subject is covered to its full. We try our best to cover every aspect of garlic, its medicinal and industrial use along with home remedies.

—Publishers

CONTENTS

GARLIC—THE WONDER FOOD

A clove of garlic a day keeps cancer away. But it does more than that.

Garlic contains a chemical called Allicin, which has already proved to have numerous health benefits. A team of Israeli scientists recently used this chemical to successfully kill cancer cells as well as malignant tumors in mice. Allicin is not present in an unbroken clove of garlic. It only gets released when the clove is crushed, so when using garlic in cooking, make sure you crush it and use it. Don't add the entire unbroken clove in your food, as though this will give you the flavour of garlic, it will not provide you with the benefits of its anti-carcinogenic properties. The clove needs to be damaged, so it is more effective crushed than cut. When crushed garlic is added to a dish, any parasites, bacteria or other microbes get killed even before the temperature kills them, so if you are worried about eating outside food—the safest option would be to order food with a strong garlic flavour. Chances of food poisoning would be slim! Garlic, as we all know or should be knowing, is a natural antiseptic, and eating a clove of garlic a day also helps ward off most infections.

Italians and Chinese eat plenty of garlic in their food, and have very low incidences of cancer. Pizzas and pastas, Italian dishes rich in maida and cheese, have liberal dozes of garlic, with the result that Italians seem relatively immune to other problems associated with such a diet such as high cholesterol and heart ailments. Similarly, Chinese food is rich in garlic, and the Chinese too are statistically less prone to cancer and heart ailments.

Needless to say, crushing a clove of garlic and eating it raw would not be the most pleasant of experiences. Garlic has a very strong flavour, and it needs to be mixed with other foods in order to be enjoyed. The best way to eat garlic would be to add it in food while cooking it. Allicin gets distributed throughout the meal, providing you with the benefits of its anti-carcinogenic and antiseptic properties.

Make sure you peel the garlic before cooking it. Cooking garlic in its peel destroys its curative properties. Similarly, peeling the garlic days before and crushing and storing all the crushed garlic together to be used a little at a time may be very convenient as a time saver, but you lose many of garlic's potent health properties. The natural compound of Allicin as found in garlic loses its beneficial properties within hours because it begins to react with garlic's other components as soon as the clove is crushed.

Peel the garlic and let it sit for fifteen minutes before cooking. Just before cooking, crush it. Consume soon after.

While you can get garlic supplements if you are looking for the easier way out, it is highly recommended that you get your daily doze of garlic the natural way—through the clove itself. As already mentioned, garlic has numerous other health benefits, and eating the garlic fresh would give you all these benefits. If you can consume the garlic raw, there's nothing like it! Peel it, crush it fifteen minutes later and down it, followed by a little milk. Do this every night—so you will not smell of garlic the entire day. Before long, you will see your health and immunity improve, and you needn't fear cancer again.

□□

GARLIC—THE MAGIC HERB

Garlic health benefits and medicinal properties have long been known. Garlic has long been considered a herbal 'wonder drug', with a reputation in folklore for preventing everything from the common cold and flu to the Plague. It has been used extensively in herbal medicine. Raw garlic is used by some to treat the symptoms of acne and there is some evidence that it can assist in managing high cholesterol levels. It can even be effective as a natural mosquito repellent.

In general, a stronger tasting clove of garlic has more sulphur content and hence more medicinal value. Some people have suggested that organically grown garlic tends towards a higher sulphur level and hence greater benefit to health. In my experience it certainly tastes better and I buy organic whenever possible.

Some people prefer to take garlic supplements. These pills and capsules have the advantage of avoiding garlic smell.

Modern science has shown that garlic is a powerful antibiotic, albeit broad-spectrum rather than targeted. The body does not appear to build up resistance to the garlic, so its positive health benefits continue over time.

Healthy Antioxidant

Studies have shown that garlic—especially aged garlic can have a powerful antioxidant effect. Antioxidants help to protect the body against damaging 'free radicals'.

Side-Effects

Raw garlic is very strong, so eating too much could produce problems, for example, irritation of or even damage to the digestive tract.

There are a few people who are allergic to garlic. Symptoms of garlic allergy include skin rash, temperature and headaches. Also, garlic could potentially disrupt anti-coagulants, so it's best avoided before surgery. As with any medicine, always check with your doctor first and tell your doctor if you are using it.

Important : A research published in 2001 concluded that garlic supplements can cause a potentially harmful side effect when combined with a type of medication used to treat HIV/AIDS.

□□

GARLIC CULTIVATION

Many people grow garlic themselves—it's easy and fun, even if you're not usually much of a gardener. You also get to the reward of eating your home-grown garlic crop!

Garlic is a member of the allium family which also includes leeks, shallots and onions. Individual cloves act as seeds. The bulbs grow underground and the leaves shoot in to the air. Although garlic is traditionally thought of as a Mediterranean ingredient, it is also grown successfully in colder more Northern climates.

There are many different garlic varieties, a lot of which you can easily grow at home for a great crop.

How to Grow Garlic at Home

Garlic is grown from the individual cloves. Each clove will produce one plant with a single bulb, which may in turn contain up to twenty cloves. Growing garlic is therefore self-sustaining.

When planting garlic, choose a garden site that gets plenty of sun and where the soil is not too damp. The cloves should be planted individually, upright and about an inch (25 mm) under the surface. Plant the cloves about 4 inches (100 mm) apart. Rows should be about 18 inches (450 mm) apart.

It is traditional to plant garlic on the shortest day of the year. Whether this is for symbolic or practical reasons is unclear.

Garlic is a very friendly plant and grows well planted with other flowers and vegetables.

Although garlic can protect other plants growing nearby against many ailments, there are some it is prone to. Garlic is also prone to a few pests.

Harvesting Your Garlic Crop

As garlic reaches maturity, the leaves will brown then die away. This is the cue that it is time to harvest your garlic crop. If you harvest too early the cloves will be very small, too late and the bulb will have split.

Proper handling of garlic after it's been picked is almost as important as looking after it whilst it's growing. It's essential that garlic is dried properly, otherwise it will rot. The bulbs are often hung up in a cool, dry place. After a week or so, take them down and brush the dirt off gently—don't wash the bulbs at this stage.

Then enjoy the delicious results of growing your own garlic in your own garden.

ORGANIC GARLIC : GOOD TO USE

Use organic ingredients, especially organic garlic, wherever possible. Organic ingredients do cost more but I think it's worth it.

Taste

There's no scientific evidence I'm aware of, yet all the anecdotal evidence is that organic foods usually taste better than the intensively farmed versions. Certainly organic onions, organic mushrooms and—of course—organic garlic all seem to benefit.

Health

All intensively farmed crops contain residues of artificial pesticides, etc. It's important to stress that these are technically safe and (usually) fall within internationally accepted levels. However some of us don't want any artifical contamination of our food. Organic Standards forbid or strictly limit the use of artificial pesticides, herbicides and fertilizers.

Environment

The issue of artificial pesticides, herbicides and fertilizers clearly has a massive effect on the environment. Organic standards support the environment by forbidding or strictly limiting their use. Instead, organic standards promote traditional farming methods such as crop rotation.

□□

VARIETIES OF GARLIC

Garlic is part of the allium genus which has around 400 varieties including onions and leeks. These include many different forms of garlic. The most commonly cultivated and eaten form of garlic is "allium sativum".

There are two sub-varieties of allium sativum: softneck garlic and hardneck garlic.

Softneck Garlic

Softneck garlic is the most commonly found. Almost all garlic available in the market is a softneck variety. This is because softneck garlic is easier to grow and plant mechanically and also keeps for longer than hardneck garlic. Softnecks are recognised by the white papery skin and an abundance of cloves, often forming several layers around the central core.

The flexible stalk also allows softneck garlic to be formed into garlic braids (plaits).

There are two main types of softneck garlic—silverskin and artichoke. Silverskin garlic is most common simply because it's easier to grow and keeps longer. Artichoke garlic tends to have fewer but larger cloves and a milder flavour. The artichoke garlic bulb wrappers are coarser than those of silverskins and sometimes have purple blotches.

Hardneck Garlic

Hardneck garlics have a 'scape'—stalk, which coils from the top. On the top of this scape grow a number of bubils which are often mistakenly referred to as garlic flowers.

Hardneck garlics have fewer, larger cloves then the

softnecks. They also have less of an outer bulb wrapper, sometimes none at all. This makes them more sensitive and reduces their shelf life.

There are three main types of hardneck garlic—rocambole, porcelain and purple stripe. Rocambole garlic usually has up to a dozen cloves of a tan or browny colour. Porcelain garlic has a satiny white wrapper and the fewest cloves in a bulb, perhaps as few as four very large cloves. Porcelain garlic is often mistaken for elephant garlic. Purple stripe garlic is highly distinctive because of its colouring, with bright purple markings.

Elephant garlic is the source of much confusion.

Many people are attracted to elephant garlic simply because of its size. They assume that it must be more strongly flavoured than ordinary garlic. In fact the opposite is true.

Elephant garlic is probably more closely related to the leek than to ordinary garlic. The bulbs are very large and can weigh over a pound. A single clove of elephant garlic can be as large as a whole bulb of ordinary garlic.

In terms of flavour, elephant garlic is to garlic what leeks are to onions. It is much less intense and sweeter. It has been described—rather unkindly—as "garlic for people who don't like garlic".

When buying elephant garlic, follow the same guidelines as ordinary garlic—look for heads that are firm with plenty of dry, papery covering. Elephant garlic is more perishable than ordinary garlic so it doesn't keep as long.

When cooking with elephant garlic, remember that it is not a substitute for ordinary garlic. Instead it is used where a subtle hint of garlic is wanted without overpowering the rest of the food. Elephant garlic is often served raw in salads or sliced and sauted in butter (be careful, it browns very quickly and can turn bitter). It's also frequently used to give a hint of flavour to soups.

□□

HOW TO TAKE GARLIC

Garlic is an important medicinal herb that is readily available everywhere, unlike some of the other herbs. It is one of the safest herbs, and as such can be taken often. It does, however, have its drawbacks, as we all know. Bear this in mind when using remedies (especially internal ones), and cut back when family and friends start avoiding you.

Garlic does indeed have scientifically-proven medicinal properties. It contains a substance called Allicin, which has anti-bacterial properties that are equivalent to a weak penicillin. It appears that cooked garlic weakens the anti-bacterial effects considerably, however, so don't count on cooked garlic with meals for much in the way of a curative.

Garlic appears to have anti-bacterial and anti-viral properties. The list is long when it comes to its uses as a remedy. This list includes wounds, ulcers, skin infections, flu, athlete's foot, some viruses, strep, worms, respiratory ailments, high blood pressure, blood thinning, cancer of the stomach, colic, colds, kidney problems, bladder problems, and ear aches, to name a few. It is believed to cure worms in both people and animals.

For most internal problems, eating garlic raw is probably the most potent way to take it. However, due to the obvious lingering odours associated with this, a tincture can be made by soaking 1/4 pound of peeled and separated garlic cloves in 1/2 quart of brandy. Seal tightly and shake every day. Strain and bottle after two weeks of this, and take in drops, 25-30 a day, if desired.

Mash 2-3 small cloves of garlic and eat it raw or boiled,

before going to sleep. You could have it with a glass of milk or with water. Avoid taking garlic in the daytime as the smell may linger.

For cough, flu, and respiratory ailments, make a cough syrup out of garlic. Slice 1 pound of fresh garlic and pour one quart of boiling water over it. Let sit for 12 hours, then add sugar until you reach the consistency of a syrup. Add honey for better taste, if desired.

For sore throat, make a garlic tea by steeping several cloves of garlic in half a cup of water overnight. Hold your nose and drink it.

Externally, garlic is a known anti-bacterial and anti-infection agent. An interesting use for ear aches is to slice a garlic clove, heat briefly in a small amount of olive oil, and let cool. Then use a drop of two in the affected ear (strain the mixture beforehand, of course).

Make an ointment out of garlic (use cloves instead of leaves, stems, or flowers as described in Ointments) for wounds, cuts, athlete's foot, or any other external skin irritation, fungus, or infection. Also, try a few drops of oil on a toothache for pain relief.

□□

HEALTH BENEFITS OF GARLIC

Modern medical discoveries have shown that, contrary to prior medical opinion, numerous diseases are caused or contributed to by infectious processes caused by bacteria or viruses, or both—gastric ulcers, ulcerative colitis, coronary artery disease and cervical cancer to name a few. Garlic may be helpful in treating or preventing some of these conditions.

Garlic's role in cancer seems to be more to prevent it than to cure it, at least based on the ways we now use it. Garlic eaters just get less cancer than non-garlic eaters, according to demographic surveys. Using garlic in various ways inhibits cancer cells from reproducing, that is, it slows down the process and may actually reverse it in the early stages.

Studies by competent multi-degreed scientists have shown beyond any reasonable doubt that consuming garlic generally has the following physical effects:

❑ Garlic lowers blood pressure a little.

❑ Garlic lowers LDL Cholesterol a little.

❑ Garlic helps reduce atherosclerotic buildup (plaque) within the arterial system. One recent study shows this effect to be greater in women than men.

❑ Garlic lowers or helps to regulate blood sugar.

❑ Garlic helps to prevent blood clots from forming, thus reducing the possibility of strokes and thromboses (It may not be good for hemophiliacs).

❑ Garlic helps to prevent cancer, especially of the digestive system, prevents certain tumors from growing larger and reduces the size of certain tumors.

❏ Garlic helps to remove heavy metals such as lead and mercury from the body.

❏ Raw garlic is a potent natural antibiotic and, while far less strong than modern antibiotics, can still kill some strains of bacteria that have become immune or resistant to modern antibiotics.

❏ Garlic has anti-fungal and anti-viral properties.

❏ Garlic dramatically reduces yeast infections due to Candida species.

❏ Garlic has anti-oxidant properties and is a source of selenium.

❏ Garlic probably has other benefits as well.

HEALING PROPERTIES OF GARLIC

Garlic actually fight off some infections that modern antibiotics can't kill. Extract of fresh garlic cloves kills or slows the growth of more than a dozen common bacteria.

If you feel like you're going to catch a cold or the flu, chew down a clove or two of garlic. If you catch an infection in its very early stage, you may not even get sick. Raw garlic seems to fight infections better than cooked garlic, but cooked garlic is good for you too. Cooked garlic may be better at protecting against heart disease. If you are bothered by garlic odour you can take the supplement tablets with an enteric coating. This coating protects the garlic, preventing it from dissolving until it reaches the intestines.

Chest Congestion

Garlic can also be helpful in clearing up chest congestion that often accompanies respiratory infections. Try this chest clearing ointment you can make yourself.

Peel and mince seven garlic cloves. Put them into a

pint-sized fruit jar; add enough shortening to cover the minced cloves. Place open jar into a pan of boiling water and let boil for three hours.

For extra effectiveness, add 1/8 teaspoon of eucalyptus oil to the melted shortening. Cool, cover and store. Rub ointment on the chest, stomach and back. Cover with a heavy bath towel. Garlic has been called the jewel among vegetables.

Other Chest Diseases

Garlic has proved effective in certain diseases of the chest. It reduces stinking of the breath in pulmonary gangrene. Garlic is also useful in the treatment of tuberculosis.

In Ayurveda a decoction of garlic boiled in milk is considered a wonderful drug for tuberculosis. One gram of garlic, 250ml of milk and a litre of water are boiled together till it reduces to one fourth of the decoction. It should be taken thrice a day. Taken in sufficient quantities, it is marvellous remedy for pneumonia.

Colds

One of the most common ailments garlic has been touted to treat is the cold. Upon the onset of the sniffles, many people testify that consuming a clove or more of raw garlic takes them away. How can a clove of garlic possibly help? Studies have shown that garlic extract improves immune function, giving our natural defence system a boost, and helping it conserve our levels of antioxidants in our system. It is this strengthening of the immune system that aids in its support for other health related conditions.

Asthma

Three cloves of garlic boiled in milk can be used every night with excellent results in asthma. A pod of garlic is peeled, crushed and boiled in 120ml pure malt vinegar. It is strained after cooling and an equal quantity of honey is mixed and preserve in a clean bottle. One or two teaspoon of this syrup can be taken with fenugreek decoction in the evening and before retiring. This has been found effective in reducing the severity of asthmatic attacks.

Heart Attack

Following a recent study a West German doctor claims that garlic may prevent heart attack. Garlic helps to break up cholesterol in the blood vessels, thereby preventing any hardening of arteries which leads to high blood pressure and heart attack. If a patient takes garlic after a heart attack, the cholesterol level comes down. Though the earlier damage may not be repaired, the chances of new attacks are reduced.

Blood Disorder

Garlic is regarded as a rejuvenator. It has been found to help remove toxins, revitalise the blood, stimulate circulation and promote colony of bacteria that prevent infection by harmful bacteria.

Skin Disorders

Garlic has been used successfully for a variety of skin disorders. Pimples disappear without a scar when rubbed with raw garlic several times a day. Even very persistance forms of acne in some adults, have been healed with garlic. Garlic rubbed over ringworm, gives quick relief. The area is burnt by the strong garlic and later the skin peels off and the ring worm is cured.

Cancer

For years research has been conducted on the effects of garlic on cancer. A healthy immune system is necessary to fight cancer, and we already know conclusively that garlic supports that system. Studies have been done on the population and in animals, as well as in test tubes. What is determined is that garlic has the ability to reduce the formation of cancerous cells. Garlic is shown to actually block cancer causing compounds from forming, and slow the growth of tumor cells. Garlic is especially helpful in blocking oesophagal, breast, stomach, prostate and bladder cancer. Research has proven that compounds in garlic not only slow the rate of growth in a tumor, but can reduce the tumor size by half. When studying the effects on breast cancer, these compounds can actually prevent carcinogens from attaching to breast cells. What are these wondrous compounds? They are diallye disulphide and s-allycystein. These compounds form when garlic is crushed. Among the sulfur components of garlic there are some called ajoenes, which are also noted for their 'anti-tumor' abilities.

Heart Disease

Just as there are many factors that cause heart disease, there are many benefits of garlic that aid in preventing and treating it. So how can garlic help keep our heart in check? First, it helps lower our cholesterol levels. It raises our HDL (good) cholesterol levels, prevents LDL (bad) cholesterol from building up on arterial walls. This reduces the chances of plaque forming in our arteries. It has also been shown to lower cholesterol levels by 9% in people who ate two cloves of garlic per day.

Recent studies have also shown it to protect the aorta. The aorta is the heart blood vessel that maintians blood pressure and flow while the heart is pumping. Age, poor diet and environmental factors such as smoking can damage the aorta, causing it to stiffen. Studies have also shown that regular consumption of garlic slows the aging of the aorta and helps keep it flexible.

Hypertension

Another heart benefit of garlic is its ability to help control our blood pressure by thinning our blood. Once again the chemical found in garlic, called ajoene, thins the blood and keeps clots from forming. Studies done with general populations have shown that where there is more garlic consumed in a population, there is also a reduced incidence of hypertension and heart disease. Although garlic's heart healthy benefits may be new to some, for centuries Chinese herbalists have been using garlic to treat people with angina attacks and circulatory disorders.

Infection

Garlic has also been known for its anti-bacterial properties. At this time Louis Pasteur discovered that bacterial cells died when they were saturated with garlic. Other cases of it being used as an antibiotic in history include WW II, when British doctors used it to treat those wounded in battle, and Albert Schweitzer used garlic to treat typhus and cholera. Garlic is known to have not only antibacterial but antiviral and antifungal abilities as well. It is effective against intestinal parasites, recurrent yeast infections and the growth candida albicans is slowed by garlic. With this in mind, it should be condsidered only as an aid to antibiotics in fighting infections, as it is not enough to replace them. Garlic can help by stimulating T-cells that help fight infection.

Impotence

Garlic has also been found to be helpful to those dealing with impotence. Folklore dating back centuries has hailed garlic as an aphrodisiac, and now studies have proven this legend to be true. We know that garlic aids in blood circulation and keeps veins and arteries youthful, but that is only one way it helps with impotence. According to researchers, to obtain an erection an enzyme is required called nitric oxide synthase, and compounds in garlic stimulate the production of this enzyme in people who suffer from low levels of it.

Pregnancy

One can also benefit from garlic during pregnancy. According to a study done by doctors in a London hospital, garlic supplementation may help weight-gain for babies that may be at risk for low birth weight. The study also found that the chance of other at-birth risk factors could be reduced, such as pre-eclampsia, which is associated with hypertension.

The list of studies involving garlic and our health could go on and on. Continuous research is being done showing the association between garlic and improved memory and learning function, as well as findings that show it can help prevent the onset of 'stress-induced hyperglycemia'. Recently, it has also been studied and found to help in detoxification of bodily systems, by increasing the levels of antioxidants in the body and decreasing the formation of toxic compounds.

So we see the many areas that garlic can help us, but what should we do now? Begin ingesting six cloves a day? First of all, one should never make changes to their lifestyle in regards to their health without consulting a physician first. Your doctor needs to know if you plan to begin supplementing garlic. If you are taking medication for high blood pressure or are scheduled for surgery, garlic intake can affect both of these things, due to its blood thinning and anticoagulative properties, so it is a must to consult with your before making any changes or additions.

Once you know it will be beneficial to you to add garlic, how should you do it? Well, most people simply like to add it to their food, but there are guidelines you should remember. One tends to reap more of garlic's benefits if it is chopped or cut. It can be added at the end of cooking, so it doesn't lose too many of its beneficial properties. Although cooking can destroy some sulfur compounds in garlic (and it is these compounds that are beneficial) it can also change the structure of some into other beneficial compounds, so you still receive the benefits of garlic, even with cooking.

Whether raw or cooked, garlic is beneficial. But some people can not tolerate the taste or the garlic breath and therefore prefer to add garlic to their diet via supplements. So how much garlic is enough? If you are taking a supplement, ask your chemist or read the label. If you are adding fresh garlic to your food, start with a little at a time as too much garlic can upset your stomach if you are not used to it.

Even starting with a little can bring you health benefits. Not only will you enjoy the zing added to your food, you can enjoy knowing you're doing something good for yourself.

Other uses

Garlic has a pronounced aphrodisiac effect. It is a tonic for the loss of sexual power from any causes. It also treats sexual debility and impotency caused by over indulgence in sex and nervous exhaustion from dissipating habit. It is said to be especially useful to old men with nervous tension and falling libido.

Garlic is the most widely used of the cultivated alliums after onions. It is used both as a food and seasoning in the preparation of soups, sauces and pickles. In Spain and Italy it is used with almost every food.

☐☐

ALWAYS HELPFUL GARLIC

Did you know that garlic contains more than 100 biologically useful chemicals, with tremendous health benefits? Here are just a few of them.

Here's why you should be munching on garlic! Pregnant? New research suggests that garlic is very beneficial if taken during pregnancy.

Pre-eclampsia

This is a condition of pregnancy when your blood pressure increases, and there is excessive protein retained in the urine. If you take garlic during pregnancy, it cuts the risk of you developing pre-eclampsia.

Boosts the baby's weight

Taking garlic boosts the weight of babies in the womb. Thus, when they are born, they are heavier than they would have been if you hadn't taken garlic. Some babies are born too small, so garlic is a definite boon in these cases.

Reduces cholesterol

Garlic plays an important role in reducing the 'bad' cholesterol in the body. There have been numerous studies of the effects of garlic on reducing cholesterol, and they have well substantiated this fact. So if you have high cholesterol, increase your garlic intake. It also helps reduce blood pressure.

Reduced risk of stroke

Reduced cholesterol and blood pressure translates into a reduced risk of heart attacks and heart diseases.

An aphrodisiac

Did you know that garlic plays the role of an aphrodisiac? Garlic improves blood circulation, and also helps prolong an erection! Great help for temporary impotence.

An anti-carcinogen

Yes, garlic also helps reduce the risk of cancer, due to its anti-carcinogenic properties. It helps prevent cancerous compounds from forming and developing into tumors. It also inhibits the growth of tumors. In fact, tumors that have already formed can be reduced by 50 to 70 percent by increasing garlic intake!

Blood clots

Garlic helps prevent blood clots from forming, and it's extremely beneficial especially if you are prone to blood clots in the legs. Garlic also helps regulate blood sugar. It is a natural antibiotic, and it has anti-fungal and anti-bacterial properties.

Precautions

Remember that although garlic is potentially beneficial for some people it is also very strong. Some people are intolerant of or even actively allergic to it.

☐ Always consult your doctor regarding any health or medical matter.

☐ The medicinal properties and benefits of garlic are strongest when it is raw and crushed or very finely chopped.

☐ Don't overdo it—too much can irritate the digestive tract.

- Raw, crushed garlic is an anti-fungal, however it can produce skin blistering.
- Raw, crushed garlic is a powerful antibiotic.
- Cooked prepared garlic is less powerful but still reputedly of benefit to the cardiovascular system.
- Garlic cloves cooked whole have very little medicinal value however their milder taste makes them more acceptable to some people.
- There have been claims that garlic can help with cholesterol management however the research is going on.
- If buying garlic pills, check the ingredients.
- Garlic should be seen a part of a healthy diet and lifestyle, not an alternative to one.
- Be aware of the possible problems with garlic.

Allicin is the most powerful medicinal compound derived from garlic and provides the greatest reputed health benefits.

Allicin does not occur in 'ordinary' garlic, it is produced when garlic is finely chopped or crushed. The finer the chopping and the more intensive the crushing, the more allicin is generated and the stronger the medicinal effect.

The technically minded might be interested in the chemistry of allicin.

As well as having antibiotic properties, allicin is an excellent anti-fungal and has been used to treat skin infections such as athlete's foot. Be cautious: too much contact with crushed garlic can result in skin blistering. You should also be aware that a few people are allergic to garlic.

Allicin starts to degrade immediately after it is produced, so its medical effectiveness decreases over time. Cooking speeds up this degradation and microwaving appears to destroy allicin totally and eliminate any health benefits.

So for the most powerful medicinal effect, crush a little raw garlic and combine with the cooked food shortly before serving. Remember that raw, crushed garlic also has the most powerful flavour!

□□

THE MEDICAL EMERGENCY AND FIRST AID USE OF GARLIC

When people have medical emergencies and there is no doctor around, a bulb of garlic can be a lifesaver—literally, if you know how to use it. Crushed raw garlic is a very powerful antibiotic, but it must be applied to the site of the infection, including staph and strep, to be effective. It will burn like fire for a minute or two but it is the best way to kill staph without a prescription medicine. Most importantly, garlic will still kill strains of staph that have become immune to modern antibiotics because it kills in a different way and the bacteria cannot become immune to it. But it must be applied in one form or another to the site of the infection.

It is best to let crushed raw garlic set for 7 or 14 minutes before using so that it can form the maximum amount of allicin in order to have greater antibacterial properties. The reason is that crushing garlic forms sulfenic acid (thus the burning sensation) which steadily breaks down into allicin, the highly antibiotic compound that kills bacteria. For reasons not clearly understood, every 6 and 1/4 minutes or so there is a rapid dramatic increase in the rate of conversion for about 30 seconds and then it drops off to normal again for another 6 and 1/4 minute cycle and then it sharply increases again for another 30 seconds or so and again drops back to the normal rate. By waiting seven minutes, you benefit from the first great wave and by waiting 14 minutes, you get the extra boost of the second surge.

Kills Bacteria

Desperate hungry survivors will eat things they never would consider normally. If there's a piece of meat that's not fresh , but you're going to cook it and eat it anyway, rub crushed garlic all over it and the garlic will kill most if not all exposed bacteria. If you eat raw garlic in the same mouthful of food with other food, it will kill some of the bacteria present, but garlic will kill a lot more if you rub it on the food before eating. Saliva deactivates allicin, as do all digestive juices and it is the allicin that kills the bacteria. If you're going to eat it anyway, at least protect yourself the best you can with garlic.

Crushed raw garlic can be used to kill bacteria and other tiny lifeforms such as E. coli in contaminated water when there is no other water available. Just crush it and let it wait as above and then mix it into a bottle of strained water and let set for an hour or two or overnight to have time to kill as many of the bacteria as possible. While it will not make the water taste any better and there may be things in it garlic doesn't work on, like oil, it's at least less toxic than before and if death is the alternative, less toxic is preferrable to more toxic. Garlic's antibiotic properties also make it useful for sterilizing things like dishes, pans, etc.

Water stabilizes allicin, the active ingredient in garlic for a while and its half-life in water is 28 days, during which time is still possesses antibiotic properties. That's important to remember. Conversely, crushed garlic left alone at room temp loses allicin rapidly the first day and gradually each day and after a week or ten days, there's little allicin left. If you only have a little, putting the crushed garlic in water will keep it useable much longer than if you just set it on a saucer.

Snake Bite

Garlic is a very old treatment for snake bite and it is supposed to work. Crush it and rub directly into and around the fang marks. It will burn like fire for a minute or two and then settle down. Most snake venom is fat soluble and therefore spreads via the lymphatic system, not the blood circulatory system—so does garlic's sulfur compounds. It should be rubbed all around the area so that it can seep into the skin and into the area's lymphatic system. Try not to move around much as movement is what causes the lymphatic fluid to flow and spread the poison. Eating garlic also helps as it gets garlic into the lymphatic system elsewhere in the body and gets it into circulation. Venomous snake bite is very serious and life threatening and garlic may not be the ideal treatment, but it's better than dying without trying anything and you might even live.

Enema

Garlic-water enema kills the bacteria that cause irritable colon and chronic diarrhoea. If a person has a bacterial infection in the colon and there is no Gastro-intestinal specialist around, then a garlic and warm water enema may prove effective in ridding the colon of the offending germs. Simply crush a couple of cloves (not bulbs or heads), wait 14 or 15 minutes or more, add to warm water, strain out the larger particles and use. Garlic that has been diluted by water is much milder and less subject to burning sensitive skin in most normal people although there may be a temporary slight burning sensation around the anus, but it's more like warming than burning. Lying on the back or the left side is a better way than sitting on a toilet because in the upright position, you only fill the descending colon but not the transverse or the ascending colon but on your back or left side, you can fill all three parts of the colon and spread garlics germ killing power throughout the entire colon. Results are usually pretty fast. It would seem beneficial to try to hold the liquid as long as one conveniently can in order for the antibiotic effect to have the best chance of working. Repeat if necessary and with an additional clove or two as needed.

If there are some bacteria in the small intestine you may not get complete relief as long as it is present. One way of dealing with it is to crush a clove of garlic and let it wait 15 minutes or more to develop more allicin and then put the crushed garlic in a spoonful of olive oil, if you're not allergic to it, and let it steep a few minutes before swallowing it. This will let it become fat-soluble so it goes out the pyloris and into the duodenum with some allicin left in it. Another way is to fill the hollowed out centre of a grape with crushed raw garlic and swallow it whole. Flushing these things down with a glass of water containing a crushed clove of garlic will help get more allicin into the stomach while adding enough water to dispel any burning sensation from the allicin or the stomach acid. The whole idea is to try to get some allicin into the small intestine so it can fight the bacteria there and help clear up the diarrhoea.

Stuffy Nose

A way to use garlic on a stuffy nose, sore throat and infection that has gone into the lungs is to crush the small end of a clove and use it like a inhaler so you breathe the fumes through your nostrils. This will help clear the passages as well as fight the germs. Eating garlic is not enough, it has to get to the site of the infection as directly as possible and breathing it in takes it all the way into the lungs. Another way to do the same thing is to crush the garlic and wrap gauze, muslin cloth or thin fabric around it and breathe through the gauze to get the vapours into the lungs. One study showed that crushed garlic vapours alone kill many kinds of bacteria. Another way is to put crushed garlic into a plastic tubing and blow air over the crushed garlic and onto a wound site that may be otherwise hard to get to. Be creative in how you use your garlicky resources, your life may be on the line.

Drug-resistant Tuberculosis

A way to break up dried lung congestion is to crush garlic, wait 14 minutes and mix it into water and strain the particles out and do reverse gargle. Take a mouthful of the garlic water, with the crushed particles strained out, and facing downward, purse your lips as if you were going to whistle and instead breathe in through your mouth so that the air bubbles in through the water and the garlic-laden moisture coats the throat and lungs and helps to break up dried phlegm as well as fighting germs.

Toothaches

If you get one of those massive brain-pounding toothaches and there's no dentist around, crushed raw garlic actually knocks out the infection and relieves pain. It has worked for me several times and all I do is to chew up the garlic some and pack the residue around the tooth. Yes, the burning sensation is quite hot and sometimes I wonder whether it is worth it but the hotness dissipates in a few minutes and the pain from the tooth lessens at the same time. There are several ways of doing this, one is to simply slice a this piece from the side of the clove and hold the cut side to the gum where the pain is and move it around the area slowly on both inside and outside gums around the affected tooth. A milder way is to take a small inner clove and cut some vertical slits in its side so a lesser amount of allicin is released but over a longer time and is still effective but takes a little longer to work. If you want the most allicin crush the clove and pack it around the tooth.

Warning : This is very hot and can irritate the skin of the gums, but this is less painful than the toothache. Basically, you trade the pain of the burning sensation of garlic for future relief of the deeper pain of the toothache. How fast you get relief is a function of how much hotness you can endure in order to get relief from toothache. Usually the pain is gone in 30 minutes to an hour and the swelling diminishes as well.

□□

ACNE TREATMENT AND GARLIC

If you have serious acne then the first thing you should do is see your doctor for advice. There are a number of powerful 'over the counter' medicines available to buy from the chemist shop that can often help to reduce symptoms. Your doctor can prescribe even more powerful and more effective products.

In terms of DIY (Do it yourself) home treatment for acne, diet is usually considered the most important. It's unlikely to be a solution on its own but might help to reduce the severity of your symptoms. The usual advice is all stuff you've heard before, but it's worth repeating: Avoid fatty and greasy foods along with processed food and refined sugars. Eat more natural whole foods including fresh fruit and vegetables. Even if bad diet isn't the cause of your acne—and there are numerous possible causes—some people believe it can make the symptoms worse.

Drinking water is particularly important, not just for acne treatment but for skin and general health. Most nutritionists agree that you should try to drink between six and eight glasses of water a day. That's pure water, nothing added. Be aware that it is possible to drink too much water, so use common sense. Water poisoning (hyperhydration) can be a serious and dangerous condition.

Is Garlic an Acne Cure?

No. Garlic won't cure the problem. The real question is whether or not it can help in controlling and reducing the severity of the symptoms.

However many people do believe it can help treat the

symptoms. It is said to do this in two ways—internal and external.

First of all, garlic has powerful antibiotic properties and is a general blood cleanser. Eating garlic might help your system internally to clean itself out and hence reduce acne symptoms. Garlic's most powerful medicinal compounds are released when it's eaten raw and crushed. A little raw garlic can be sprinkled on top of a meal at the end of cooking, added to a salad, included in a sandwich, etc. Be warned that the taste and the smell of raw garlic is very strong.

The antibiotic and cleansing properties of garlic also give it a reputation in folk medicine as being an effective acne treatment when a little is applied gently externally. However although some people seem to think it works, others have reported nothing other than skin burning and reddening.

As always, consult your doctor before attempting any home treatment.

□□

GARLIC WATER AND ITS USE

There are two excellent ways of using garlic's antibiotic properties that can be very helpful in getting garlic to places where there are infections, one is the crushed raw garlic enema discussed in the previous chapter and the other is the garlic bath, including the garlic sitz-bath for combating pelvic fungal infections. It doesn't take much garlic, just a few cloves from a bulb is plenty for most applications and it's dosage related so you can always increase the amount of garlic if you are fighting a more persistent adversary. A little garlic can go a long way, it can be a matter of how long you let it set after crushing and before adding to water and then using. Garlic water that has set for a few days can be extremely strong smelling and I regard that as a way of estimating that is has increased in potency.

Because of the wide range of tastes and flavours in garlics and the proclivity of the hotter ones to burn tender skin, I think it is smart to start out with the milder ones so as not to burn sensitive internal tissue and I did. Also because of garlic waters tendency to increase in potency with time, I used fairly fresh garlic waters and found them to be very effective in getting results that made me feel better. For me, feeling better is what it's all about.

Garlic baths and enemas are very important tools in that they are about the only ways to get allicin inside the human body without it going through the chemical changes imposed by the digestive process. Allicin, which is both fat and water-soluble, cannot exist for long in the human body and has a half-life of less than one minute in blood before being changed into other things, and scientists currently do not know what those other things are or how they fit in. Because allicin kills germs differently than standard antibiotics, it is one of the most powerful antibiotics in nature if you can get it into contact with the staph, strep etc. A garlic-water enema puts it directly in the colon while still in it's most potent antibacterial form and it can kill a lot of bacteria in there.

Water doesn't completely stop sulfenic acid from breaking down into allicin, it just slows it down greatly but the solution continues to increase in allicin the longer it sets and after a few days produces such an intense odour that I would be afraid to use it without diluting it greatly. My suspicion is that it would make a great external application antibiotic. The way garlic continuously changes makes it difficult to prescribe any kind of accurate dosage.

Garlic water doesn't require refrigeration but it can get pretty pungent after a few days and probably highly antibiotic but smells to bad I would be afraid to use it for any internal use. I would like to see more research into this. I once soaked my feet in three day-old garlic water and it really made me feel good and knocked out the athlete's foot fungus on the right foot and the toenail fungus on the left foot. I will bathe my feet in garlic water about once a month or so and let you know about the toenail fungus as the new toenails grow out.

Another use of garlic water is that it can probably deliver usable amounts of allicin to fight bacteria in the stomach. The water that carries the allicin thins out the stomach acids, slowing down the rate at which it neutralizes the allicin and allowing some of it to kill bacteria and also the water, by thinning out the stomach acids, reduces the pain some people feel when they eat raw garlic. Because it is waterborne, some of its compounds can pass through the capillary walls and get into the bloodstream along with the H_2O and have some beneficial effects. In the bloodstream garlic compounds won't last long before being pounced upon by the immune system, which will use these compounds to strengthen itself by making antibodies, for example.

Chemically, an interesting thing about garlic water is that it has both water-soluble and fat-soluble compounds and they work their way through the body in different way with the water-solubles going via the venous system whereas the fat-solubles enter through and travel via the lymphatic system.

If your house has a foul odour, even after you clean the mud out, garlic can actually be used as a house deodorant and fumigant, believe it or not. I have used this method of overcoming the smell when a mouse died in an inaccessible area in a closet and it worked well both times to overcome the foul odours. Break several bulbs into cloves and crush the cloves and leave them all about the place (on saucers or paper plates) and then close it up for the night. When you come back the next day, the garlic will probably be the dominant odour, but that's usually preferable to a sewage or rotting smell. Leave in place as long as necessary. Usually as the odour of garlic diminishes over a few days, the other odour is gone, too. If not, treat again, with more garlic if needed. Of course to be truly effective, you have to remove the source of the foul smell or it will continue to produce the offending odour.

□□

LITTLE KNOWN SECRETS TO USE GARLIC IN COOKING

Many people love the wonderful thing fresh garlic can do to enliven an otherwise unremarkable dish. Some like the flavour but fear the dreaded social curse of garlic breath. Others fear garlic may overpower an otherwise delicately flavoured work of culinary art. Put your concerns to rest, epicures, there are ways to deal effectively with these and other aspects of natures best health food to add life to your creations by creating just the right amount of flavour. Conversely, we will also pass along ways to embolden ethnic dishes and others so as to enhance the depth and breath of their central flavour, that of garlic.

❐ Many factors influence how much flavour is imparted to a dish by the garlic. You can actually make a mild garlic seem much more potent and a powerful garlic seem meek, just by knowing how to prepare the garlic and when to add it to the food you are preparing. A properly cured, healthy garlic bulb has neither smell nor taste, nor does a carefully removed clove from the bulb. You can gently peel the clove cover away from a clove and it still has no taste or smell, unless you damage it in some way during the separating or peeling process. The reason for this is the components of garlic that cause its smell and taste are kept apart by the internal and external cellular walls.

When garlics cellular walls are broken by damaging the clove, the alliin and allinase that are stored apart from each other in the clove mix together and form the allicin, which is what causes garlic to smell and taste as it does.

Allicin is a volatile substance that will break down on its own in a few hours and form several different sulphuric compounds. Heating allicin will cause it to break down much faster. The more allicin breaks down, the less of the smell and taste are present. Therein lies the second of the secrets to using garlic.

❏ Peeling individual cloves can be tedious, especially if the clove covers are tight. There's an easy way—just soak the cloves to be peeled in plain water for an hour or two beforehand and those clove covers will zip right off easily and without damaging the clove. It is fast and odourless, indicating it does not harm the clove. It looks like a large piece of pasta and you just put one or more cloves in there, roll it against a hard surface and the clove covers split right open.

If you wish a more subtle garlic presence in your preparation, either put the cloves in whole or cut them into thick slices and cook them longer. You can put a big handfull of whole garlic cloves in a small pot of soup and hardly even know there's any garlic in it. The more you cut the garlic, the more of the allicin is formed and the stronger the flavour. If you cut a clove into 8 slices, it will have more flavour than if you cut it into only 4 slices. If you dice the clove into many small cubes, it will release even more flavour and if you crush it, you will release the most flavour.

If you want to bring out the full flavour of crushed garlic, let it set a few minutes to steep before adding it to your dish at the end of its cooking time.

To remove garlic odour from the hands, just rub the hands with a piece of stainless steel flatware under running water and most of the smell magically goes away.

❏ Timing is important. When you put the garlic into the food you are cooking makes a huge difference in its eventual taste. The longer you cook the garlic, the less it will taste and smell and the more creamy and subtle its flavour becomes. If you want just a hint of garlic essence, use a mild variety of garlic in either whole cloves or thick slices and put them in early in the cooking process. If you use crushed garlic, there is more allicin to dissipate, but the result will be a richer, creamier garlic taste. Even a large, powerful garlic can be tamed by cooking it for longer than you otherwise would. If you want your creation to be bold, powerful and fairly reek of garlic, crush the cloves and put them in just before the cooking is complete and you are almost ready to remove it from the fire. Even a mild garlic will seem more potent when used this way.

❑ If you wish to eat a lot of garlic for its health benefits without being overpowered by it, you can put a whole bulb or more in a soup or stew of your choosing and get almost all of those benefits, and plenty of them, and still have a mild tasting dish. All you have to do is peel all of the cloves and slice them and put the slices into the soup at the beginning of cooking. You'll be pleasantly surprised at how mild 25 or 30 cloves of garlic can be when prepared this way. You almost can't taste them but your body will still get the healthful benefits from the garlic. You can also add them in this way to rice, beans, pasta sauces, scalloped potatoes or almost any dish you like.

If you eat any fried or fatty foods or meats, you owe it to yourself to have garlic in some form with that meal to help counteract the elevated cholesterol that can otherwise come from such a meal. I remember seeing a study done at a clinic where a large number of people were fed a fatty meal, all getting the same sized portions, but some contained garlic and some did not. Those who had garlic in their meal had normal cholesterol readings after the meal. Those who did not get garlic had raised cholesterol readings. Think about it.

Whole cloves of garlic that have been cooked until they are mushy have no discernable health benefits as the cooking process destroys the enzyme, alliinase, before it can form allicin. The only exceptions are where the cloves are not yet cooked all the way through, that is if there is still a firm inner core that has crispness and pungency, or hotness. If you want health benefits, don't cook the whole cloves until they are mushy, leave some firmer inner cores and you will not only get some health benefits, but a surprisingly delicious eating experience as the heat takes a lot of the edge off the garlic and smoothes out the taste a lot while at the same time giving you something that is delightfully crunchy and warm in the centre of the sweet mushy garlic clove.

□□

ALLICIN—The most potent medicinal
COMPOUND OF GARLIC

The most potent medicinal compound derived from garlic is allicin and it is for this that most people turn to garlic supplements. The chemistry of allicin is complex—it is not present in natural garlic but is released when garlic is crushed. In addition, allicin is unstable and breaks down quickly. Producing garlic supplements that will release significant quantities of allicin is not easy. This might explain their price.

There's no clear consensus on which products are best. One rule of thumb when buying garlic supplements is to check the label for the amount of allicin released. Use this information to compare different brands. The amount of allicin—if any—depends on the production method. Some people are sceptical that odourless capsules can contain any allicin—after all, it is the sulphorous compounds such as allicin that give garlic its smell in the first place.

Be aware that some garlic supplements list the amount of alliin they contain. That one letter difference is important—it isn't a spelling mistake! Alliin is a precursor compound to allicin however conversion rate between alliin and allicin is extremely variable. On its own an alliin figure is of little value.

Of all garlic's reputed medicinal benefits, perhaps the most well known is its use as a natural antibiotic with reports going back through history. There are even stories of garlic being used to ward off the plague. It's not known how effective this was, however there is some evidence that anthrax is sensitive to garlic. Some people have even suggested that it might help in the fight against acne although that might be too much to hope for.

Garlic's antibiotic properties have been more extensively studied than some of its other reputed health benefits. Louis Pasteur examined garlic's use as an antibacterial back in the nineteenth century and showed how it killed bacteria under laboratory conditions. Numerous modern studies confirm that garlic has definite antibiotic properties and is effective against many bacteria, fungi and viruses.

Researchers have compared the effectiveness of garlic with that of commercial prescription antibiotics. The result is often that garlic is more effective as a broad spectrum antibiotic. However if a particular bacterium or virus is being treated a more specifically targeted antibiotic could be a more effective treatment than garlic.

One significant advantage of garlic is that the body does not seem to build up a resistance to it as it does to many modern antibiotics. This also makes it potentially effective against hospital superbugs.

Note : Garlic can interfere with the operation of some medical drugs, in particular anti-coagulants. I do not advocate taking garlic before entering hospital unless you discuss it with your doctor first.

The antibiotic properties of garlic are a direct result of the allicin produced from raw, crushed garlic. This is destroyed by age and cooking—cooked garlic has virtually no antibiotic value although it still retains other benefits.

I do not recommend garlic as a replacement for conventional antibiotics unless agreed with your doctor. However as more and more antibiotics are becoming useless due to over-prescription and side effects, garlic could have a place to play in modern medicine.

❐❐

THE GARLIC ANTIBIOTIC

This is where garlic could come in. Garlic is a broad spectrum antibiotic with powerful antibacterial properties.

In general antibiotics are ineffective against viral infections of the sort that cause most colds and flu. Fortunately garlic isn't 'just' an antibiotic. As well as the powerful antibacterial allicin, garlic produces a number of other potentially beneficial compounds.

It seems that garlic can have positive effects for the immune system as a whole. In this way it might indirectly help the body to fight off illnesses for which modern antibiotics would be inappropriate. Many herbal supplements on the market contain garlic, often along with other traditional herbs.

Garlic is sometimes said to help treat the symptoms of colds and flu, however it is best seen as a preventative. The use of garlic against colds and flu seems to be most effective when taken before the infection is caught, or immediately the symptoms begin to show.

Scientific research has shown that people taking garlic can suffer less from colds than a control group. There is also plentiful anecdotal evidence that taking large amounts of garlic at the onset of a cold can reduce the time taken to recover.

Colds and flu are a 'moving target'. A treatment aimed at one type of cold or flu can often be of no use in treating the others.

GARLIC ALLERGY

Garlic is generally lauded as a health giving herb, however as with almost any food there are a number of people who are intolerant or allergic to it.

Symptoms & Intolerance

Even if you don't have an explicit allergy to garlic, too much exposure to allicin (produced when garlic is crushed) can cause similar symptoms. These include skin irritation, reddening and even blistering. Low level intolerance or excessive intake can result in heartburn or flatulence.

A few people do have an actual allergy to garlic. Symptoms vary but often include stomach problems after eating garlic and a rash from eating or from physical contact.

Garlic allergy has also been reported to exacerbate asthma symptoms, though this is more usually related to breathing in garlic dust rather than eating garlic.

Even if you are not normally allergic or sensitive to garlic, eating an unusually large amount can produce similar reactions. A large amount of raw garlic could irritate and possibly even damage the digestive tract. Garlic is powerful and as with anything powerful it should be treated with respect.

All allergies can be potentially serious. If you suspect that you might be suffering from garlic allergy—or any other sort, food or otherwise—you should contact your doctor or a medically qualified clinic to arrange for testing.

□□

HOW TO GET RID OF GARLIC-BREATH

Despite the many culinary and health benefits of garlic there is one serious drawback—it's hard to prevent garlic breath. The more you enjoy garlic, the more of it you are likely to consume and the worse the garlic breath problem is likely to become.

One unfortunate facet of bad breath is that you can rarely smell it yourself. If you eat a lot of garlic then it is probably safest to assume that you do have garlic breath, even if your friends are too polite to mention it!

Many substances cause breath problems. One of the reasons that garlic breath is so strong is that garlic is full of sulphorous compounds. These compounds 'feed' the bacteria in the mouth and bad breath (halitosis) is caused as a result.

If you have bad breath generally then you probably have a lot of these halitosis inducing bacteria in your mouth anyway and so will suffer more from the effects of garlic.

Is there a Cure?

The only guaranteed way to prevent garlic breath is simply not to eat garlic! For some of us that is inconceivable. However, if your main reason for eating garlic is for the health benefits then you could consider switching to odourless garlic supplements instead.

Unfortunately there's no way of getting rid of the symptoms of garlic eating totally. You can reduce and mask the smell of your breath, but garlic still works its way through your entire system. So even with a powerful bad breath cure the garlic will usually still emerge from your pores the next day. A true garlicophile can literally 'seep' garlic through the skin.

That said, there are some ways that the problems can at least be reduced.

How to Get Rid of this Problem

Bacteria induced garlic breath can be reduced by usual oral hygine methods. Standard halitosis remedies include regular use of mouthwash, brushing and flossing teeth and tongue scraping.

There are also commercial bad breath remedies available which are more powerful than the usual mouthwashes you can buy in supermarkets. These are available from your doctor, your pharmacist or to buy online.

Another method of reducing garlic breath is to eat parsley with the meal. This seems to counteract the problem to some extent, although it doesn't prevent it completely. It's probably no coincidence that many garlic recipes also contain parsley. However it is not enough just to sprinkle in a teaspoon of dried parsley when cooking. To get the effect you need to chew at least one sprig of fresh parsley, preferably more. Ideally this should be chopped and added near the end of cooking.

Some people also claim that chewing cardamom seeds has a similar effect to parsley and can work as a garlic breath remedy. Cardamom has a very strong flavour so this might not be an option for some people.

❏❏

FREQUENTLY ASKED QUESTIONS

Now, it is turn for few questions and there answers that generally hit the reader's mind.

Is there more than one kind of garlic?

Yes, there are hundreds of local garlics from all over the world and they all derive from 17 basic kinds that fall into three types of Hardnecks and two types of Softneck garlics.

Does all garlic taste the same?

No, some are very mild and some are very strong and there is every taste level in between.

Does cooked garlic have the same benefits as raw garlic?

As near as I can figure out, you lose very little in cooking it. The first thing you would lose would be the allicin and its antibiotic properties. Heat breaks it down rather quickly, as do digestive chemicals. What it breaks down into; however, is a soup of sulphur compounds that are antibiotic also. Most of the health benefits from garlic come from the breakdown compounds, rather than allicin itself, anyway, as allicin breaks down in the body and it is the breakdown components that get into the bloodstream. They're the ones that really do most of the good.

Cooked garlic would seem to have less immediate antibiotic value. Doctors have indicated that the smellier the garlic, the better it works, as the smelly compounds seem to do the most work. Some of the helpful compounds are probably destroyed during the cooking process and dissipate in the form of cooking odours. On the plus side, you can eat a lot more cooked garlic than you can raw garlic, at least most people can. I usually eat a clove or two raw with cooked meals, anyway. I suspect that you do lose a little with cooking, but are able to make up for it by being able to eat more of it.

How can I dry garlic at home?

The best way is to peel the cloves (tight clove covers). Soak them for an hour or more in water—they'll slip right off) then cut the cloves into 1/8th inch thick slices. Lay these slices out to dry on a perforated surface such as 1/4 inch cloth or screen. If using a dehydrator, use the lowest temperature setting.

What is round or ball garlic?

What you seem to have gotten are garlic rounds. As garlic goes through the development underground from a clove to a fully cloved bulb, it first swells into a large round undivided ball with a lot of wrappers that are almost fused together. As it grows, it begins to divide and sub-divide into as many cloves as it can before the heat causes it to lose its leaves. If the temperature increases before the garlic has time to divide, then the result is a large undivided round. Every time we harvest we find some of them. If replanted as is in the fall, they will form large fully divided bulbs the following spring. These rounds have the same taste and other properties as the clove they came from. Mild tasting garlics yield mild tasting rounds and strong garlics result in strong tasting rounds. For spring planting, rounds are your best bet to produce a good size bulb by the time early summer heat forces maturity.

From a cook's standpoint, one large cloves means a lot less peeling, etc. Also, they seem to keep much longer than fully developed garlic, probably due to that heavy, thick wrapper they have.

What is that garlic that looks like green onions? Is it all edible?

What you have is green garlic, a delightful harbinger of spring to bring fresh young garlic flavour so delicately to the fortunate palate of one so lucky as to find these special treats. Yes, the entire plant can be eaten, though the roots would be a bit stringy and should be trimmed off. Growers often cull out small plants that lag the others and would result in small garlic and sell them as green garlic, much in the way the onion grower sells green onions. They're generally only available in the spring and not very widely marketed, most people have never tried them.

Slices of green garlic light up a cheese omelette and can also give a heady lift to new potato soup. Try them in stews or stir-fry for a special treat. Green garlic is very mild but still has a marvelous essence of garlic that is uplifting. They're also excellent eaten raw as an adjunct to a sandwich or a bowl of soup.

How long should garlic store?

Some varieties naturally store longer than others, but most should be able to store at ordinary room temperature for at least 6 months after it comes out of the ground is not unreasonable. Early harvesting varieties seem to store less long than the later maturing varieties, but it's just that they've been out of the ground longer. Rocamboles are the shortest storing garlics, typically 5-6 months. Silverskins, like Locati store 8 to 10 months, and Creole Silverskins like Burgundy store 8-9 months. Purple Stripes like Metechi and Chesnok Red store 7-8 months. If garlic has been stored in refrigeration, it will have a very short storage life after it comes out of the fridge. Most grocery store garlic has been stored under refrigeration for weeks or months before being put on the shelf and as a result, deteriorates within weeks.

How should garlic be stored?

I think unglazed terra cotta works best. Those little garlic keepers are excellent for just a few bulbs. You could also use terra cotta flower pots. Or, you could store garlic in an open brown paper bag or a paper fiber egg carton or a cardboard box—allow for air circulation and keep it out of direct sunlight as that will dry it out faster. Net bags work very well as long as there's not so much garlic in them as to impair air circulation. DO NOT STORE GARLIC IN PLASTIC OR ANY AIRTIGHT CONTAINER. I don't recommend storing garlic in the refrigerator because the humidity can induce fungal and bacterial problems and the low temperature can cause early sprouting.

Can you plant garlic in the spring?

Yes it can, but it seldom gives as good results as fall-planted garlic because it does not have enough time to develop fully and may result in small bulbs or undivided rounds.

Do all garlics mature and harvest at the same time?

No. It is usually 6 to 8 weeks from the time the earliest variety (Turban or Asiatic Artichokes—such as Chinese Purple or Asian Rose) is harvested until the time the last variety (Silverskins, like Locati) is taken out of the ground. Most garlics harvest somewhere in mid season. The larger they are, the longer it takes them to cure, that is dry down.

□□

GARLIC RECIPES

These garlic bites are a simple variation on the traditional cheese straws. If you can make pastry then these are very easy.

Garlic bites can be served either as a pre-dinner appetiser or as a party snack.

GARLIC BITES

This recipe makes about 64 garlic bites. That sounds a lot but they disappear quicker than a vampire on midsummer's day!

120gm	Self-Raising Flour
60gm	Butter
60gm Cheese, grated	Use any strong, sharp cheese
2 Cloves Garlic, crushed	As always, adjust garlic according to taste
1/2 tsp Dry Mustard Powder	
1 tbsp Cold Water	
Salt	Use a little more or less as needed

❐ Sift the flour into a bowl. Mix in the mustard powder and the crushed garlic.

❐ Cut the butter and slowly rub into the flour. Add a little cheese now again as you go along. Continue to combine the ingredients, adding a little cold water at the end if necessary to get a nice lump of pastry dough.

- [ ] Place the pastry in the fridge to rest for 15 minutes or so. Meanwhile heat the oven to 200 C (400 F).
- [ ] Roll out the pastry on a lightly floured board to form a square about 8 inches (16 cm) each side. With a sharp knife divide the pastry into eighths in each direction to give 64 small squares.
- [ ] Transfer the squares to a greased baking tray, arranging the garlic bites with a little space between them. Grind a little salt across the tops.
- [ ] Bake for 10 to 15 minutes. Remove and allow to cool.
- [ ] Transfer the garlic bites to an airtight container, they'll keep for a day or two.

GARLIC CHICKEN

Some garlic chicken recipes involve roasting a whole chicken. That's great, if you've got both the time and enough people to eat the chicken!

This simple garlic chicken recipe uses chicken breast and serves two. It makes a quick and easy garlic chicken supper.

15gm Butter

1 tbsp Olive Oil

1 Onion, finely chopped

2 Cloves Garlic, crushed   As always, adjust garlic according to taste

2 Chicken Breasts

280 ml Chicken Stock

Salt and Pepper

Handful fresh Parsley, chopped

2 tbsp Natural Yoghurt

- [ ] Trim the chicken and cut into bite-sized pieces.
- [ ] Melt the butter in a pan, add the olive oil. Add the

chopped onions and cook gently until soft and golden. Add the garlic and cook for another minute or so.

◻ Add the chicken pieces to the onion and garlic mixture and brown on all sides.

◻ Add the chicken stock, season with salt and pepper to taste and add the chopped parsley. Bring to the boil then turn the heat down to minimum and leave gently cooking—uncovered—for about 20 minutes.

◻ Remove the chicken pieces and keep warm. Turn up the heat and reduce the liquid by about half. Remove from the heat and stir in the yoghurt.

◻ Serve the garlic chicken with mashed potato, your favourite veg and the garlicky sauce.

GARLIC MUSHROOM

If you love both garlic mushrooms and garlic chicken then this recipe's for you. Chicken breast stuffed with garlic mushrooms—a great tasting recipe that's a lot easier to prepare than it looks.

For a massive garlic hit you could even serve this with white garlic sauce.

2 Large Chicken Breasts

120gm Mushrooms — Chestnut mushrooms have a lovely flavour however ordinary mushrooms will do just as well

15gm Butter

2 Cloves Garlic, crushed — As always, adjust garlic according to taste

15gm Breadcrumbs

Handful fresh Parsley, chopped

Handful fresh Coriander leaves, chopped

Salt & pepper

☐ Wash the mushrooms then chop small. It'll look as if you've got enough to feed a party but don't worry, they'll reduce down.

☐ Melt the butter in a pan, add the garlic and cook gently for a few seconds, then add the mushrooms and stir well. Cook over a medium heat for about ten minutes, stirring occasionally.

☐ At first the mushrooms will release a lot of liquid, most of this will evaporate away in the latter half of the cooking.

☐ Whilst the mushrooms are cooking, pre-heat the oven to 200C (400F).

☐ Stir the herbs into the garlic mushrooms and season with a little salt and a generous helping of freshly ground black pepper. Add the breadcrumbs to soak up the remaining liquid. Mix together to form a paste—the stuffing. Remove from the heat and leave to cool.

☐ Cut a deep slit in each chicken breast and insert half the garlic mushroom stuffing into each one. Use a couple of cocktail sticks to close the chicken up, fold the ends over the top and use another cocktail stick or two to close the parcel up.

☐ Transfer the garlic mushroom stuffed chicken parcels to an ovenproof dish, the slit side uppermost. Cook for about 25 mins or until the chicken is properly done.

☐ Serve the garlic mushroom chicken either with traditional potatoes and veg or on a bed of lightly spiced rice. Remember to remove the cocktail sticks before serving!

GARLIC TOMATO SAUCE

This simple tomato garlic sauce is extemely flexible.

Served hot it makes a perfect pasta sauce (the amount here will serve two). Left to cool this garlic sauce makes a great substitute for ordinary ketchup or a garlicky dip.

1 Large Onion, finely chopped

4 Cloves Garlic, crushed   As always, adjust garlic
according to taste

1 Glass Dry White Wine

400gm Tin Chopped
Tomatoes

1 tbsp Tomato Puree
(paste)

1 tbsp Dried Mixed Herbs

1 tsp Lemon Juice

Salt & Pepper

☐ Heat a little oil in a pan and cook the onion for a few minutes until softened. Add the crushed garlic and cook for another minute.

☐ Pour in the wine, turn up the heat and reduce the volume by about half. Turn down the heat, add the other ingredients and stir well. Use salt and pepper according to taste.

☐ Turn the heat down to absolute minimum and cook the sauce gently for about 15 minutes, stirring occasionally.

☐ The tomato garlic sauce should now be the right consistency to serve with pasta. If you want to use it as a ketchup or a dip then cook for a few minutes more to make it slightly thicker.

☐ Serve the garlic tomato sauce warm immediately with pasta, or allow to cool then store in the fridge to use as a ketchup or a garlicky tomato dip.

WHITE GARLIC SAUCE

This garlic flavoured white sauce has many uses. Mash some garlic sauce in with freshly boiled potatoes for a lovely garlic mashed potato recipe. Use the sauce for steak or instead of ketchup with sausages or burgers. Make up a large batch of it and use as a dipping sauce at your next barbeque. This garlic sauce is extremely versatile.

45gm Butter

1 Onion, finely chopped

2 Cloves Garlic, crushed   As always, adjust garlic according to taste

1 Glass Dry White Wine

Salt and Pepper

30gm Flour

280 ml Milk

❒ Melt 15gm butter in a pan, add the chopped onions and cook gently until soft and golden. Add the garlic and cook for another minute or so. Season with salt and pepper to taste. Add the wine, turn up the heat and reduce the volume by about half. Remove from heat.

❒ In another pan melt the remaining 30 gm of butter. Add the flour, stir and cook for about five minutes.

❒ Now add the milk. If you've never made a white sauce before, the key is: take it slowly. Add just a little milk, stir well, then a little more. At first the result will look like a pastry. After a little more milk it will resemble an elastic dough. Beat this smooth. Then as you add the rest of the milk a little at a time keep stirring You'll end up with a nice thick sauce.

❒ Mix in the onion and garlic and you're done.

❒ Serve the garlic sauce warm.

❒❒

GARLIC PILLS & CAPSULES

Eating lots of garlic isn't always practical or socially desirable. There are even some people who don't like the taste!

The main reason for not eating lots of garlic is usually the fear of garlic breath. Unfortunately there are no odourless varieties of garlic available. For this reason many people prefer to buy odourless garlic supplements. These are widely available and come in various forms, the most usual being pills and capsules.

GARLIC PILLS-CAPSULES

So do they work? Do garlic supplements provide the health benefits of garlic? Is taking a dietary capsule good for your health or just a waste of money?

As is so often the case, the answer is 'it depends'. Garlic supplements vary greatly. As with all medicines, consult your doctor before taking garlic supplements. In particular garlic should be avoided by those about to undergo surgery as it can disrupt anti-coagulants.

The most potent medicinal compound derived from garlic is allicin and it is for this that most people turn to garlic supplements. The chemistry of allicin is complex—it is not present in natural garlic but is released when

59

garlic is crushed. In addition, allicin is unstable and breaks down quickly. Producing garlic supplements that will release significant quantities of allicin is not easy. This might explain their price.

There's no clear consensus on which products are best. One rule of thumb when buying garlic supplements is to check the label for the amount of *allicin* released. Use this information to compare different brands. Other figures such as 'equivalent to x cloves' are not so important. The amount of allicin depends on the production method. Some people are sceptical that odourless capsules can contain *any* allicin, it is the sulphorous compounds such as allicin that give garlic its smell in the first place.

Even without allicin, capsules might still be of value to some people because of the other sulphides they contain. In particular there has been a lot of research into the possible beneficial effects of aged garlic extract.

If you want to take nutritional garlic supplements, then to get the best medicinal benefits you should go for quality and always check the allicin level on the packet. Even without allicin content, garlic capsules might be of value to some people. Always check with your doctor, especially if you are taking other medication or are due to undergo surgery.

□□

SIDE EFFECTS OF GARLIC

Even though garlic is natural, it is not always free of side effects. For most people, these garlic side effects are merely bothersome. However, garlic can sometimes cause serious side effects as well, especially when taken at higher dosages, such as when garlic is used medicinally.

Many people may experience gastrointestinal side effects from garlic, such as:

☐ Garlicky breath or body odour

☐ Heartburn or indigestion

☐ Mouth irritation or burning

☐ Gas

☐ Nausea

☐ Vomiting

☐ Diarrhoea

These bothersome side effects are more commonly seen when raw garlic is used. 'Odourless' garlic supplements are available, but there is some concern that these products may not contain enough of the active components of garlic to provide any benefit.

Serious Garlic Side Effects

There are a number of side effects with garlic that you should report to your doctor and which might indicate that you should stop taking it.

☐ Any unusual bruising or bleeding (garlic can increase the risk of bleeding)

☐ Black, tarry stools; bright red blood in the stool; or vomiting of blood (signs of gastrointestinal bleeding)

☐ Signs of a hemorrhagic stroke (bleeding in the brain), such as:

- Vision or speech changes
- Weakness or numbness in an arm or leg
- Severe headache

☐ Signs of an allergic reaction, such as:

- An unexplained rash
- Hives
- Itching
- Unexplained swelling
- Wheezing
- Difficulty in breathing or swallowing

If you think you are experiencing a garlic side effect, please let your doctor know. Also, let your doctor know if you develop something that 'just does not seem right.' While it may not be a side effect of garlic, your doctor will be able to diagnose and treat the problem.

☐☐☐

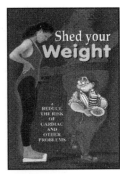

Set of
Small Size
ENGLISH
GENERAL BOOKS

❏ Home Gardening	50.00
❏ 101 Feng Shui Tips	50.00
❏ 101 Vastu Tips	50.00
❏ Dadi Maa's Home Remedies	50.00
❏ Pregnancy & Child Care	40.00
❏ Baby Health & Child Care	40.00
❏ All About Yoga	40.00
❏ Diabetes Cause & Cure	40.00
❏ Hypertension Cause & Cure	40.00
❏ Shed Your Weight	40.00
❏ How to Increase Your Height	40.00
❏ How to Increase Sex Power	40.00

SET OF SMALL ENGLISH JOKE BOOKS

❏ Juicy Joke Book (Surendra Mohan Pathak)	50.00
❏ Midnight Jokes	30.00
❏ Party Jokes	30.00
❏ Naughty Jokes	30.00
❏ Spicy Jokes	30.00
❏ Tickling Jokes	30.00
❏ Superhit Jokes	30.00
❏ Non-Veg Jokes	30.00
❏ International Jokes	30.00
❏ SMS Jokes	30.00
❏ Internet Jokes	30.00

MANOJ PUBLICATIONS
761, Main Road Burari, Delhi-110084.
Ph. No. : 27611116, 27611349   Fax : 27611546

RUCHI MEHTA'S COOK BOOK SERIES

- ❏ Dal Curries & Pulao — 40.00
- ❏ Ice Creams, Cakes & Puddings — 40.00
- ❏ Aaloo Paneer Dishes — 40.00
- ❏ Rajasthani Khaana — 40.00
- ❏ Pickles Chutenies & Murabbe — 40.00
- ❏ Vegetarian Cook Book — 40.00
- ❏ Punjabi Khaana — 40.00
- ❏ Breakfast Specialists — 40.00
- ❏ Laziz Mughalai Khaana — 40.00
- ❏ Delicious Soups — 40.00
- ❏ South Indian Food — 40.00
- ❏ Party Cooking — 40.00
- ❏ Tasty Snacks — 40.00
- ❏ Microwave Cooking — 40.00
- ❏ Chatpati Chaat — 40.00
- ❏ Non Vegetarian Food — 40.00
- ❏ Gujrati Dishes — 40.00
- ❏ Vegetarian Chinese Foods — 40.00
- ❏ Non Vegetarian Chinese Foods — 40.00
- ❏ Zero Oil Cooking — 40.00

MANOJ PUBLICATIONS
761, Main Road Burari, Delhi-110084.
Ph. No. : 27611116, 27611349   Fax : 27611546